ISBN 1 85854 145 X
Published by Brimax Books Ltd, Newmarket, England 1994.
Printed in Spain.

Learn with Teddy

ABC · 123
Words · Rhymes

Illustrated by
Ann and Mike
Ricketts

Brimax . Newmarket . England

Aa

A is for acrobat
Tumbling across the floor;
The teddies clap together
And loudly cheer for more.

Bb

B is for bicycle,
The teddies like to ride;
They race each other down the path
Then cycle side by side.

Cc

C is for cat
High up on the wall;
Sam wants to stop and say, "Hello!"
But he is far too small.

Dd

D is for dolphin
Swimming in the sea;
The teddies watch him play all day,
As happy as can be.

Ee

E is for elephant
Living at the zoo;
The teddies like to watch him
As he eats the whole day through!

Ff

F is for fair,
The teddies have such fun;
They ride upon the merry-go-round
And wave to everyone.

11

Gg

G is for gloves
Ben wears in the snow;
He likes to watch his friends
As they're skating to and fro.

Hh

H is for holly
Above the Christmas tree;
Sam is wrapping presents
For his friends, on Christmas Eve.

13

Ii

I is for igloo
Made on a snowy day;
The teddies put on hats and scarves
Then run outside to play.

Jj

J is for juggler
Throwing balls so high;
The teddy bears all sit and watch
As they seem to touch the sky.

15

Kk

K is for kangaroo
Bouncing all around;
The teddies like to watch him
Jump high up off the ground.

L is for lake
Where the teddies like to be;
They watch the boats go sailing by
As happy as can be.

Mm

M is for mouse
That runs across the floor;
Rosie tries to catch him
As he slips out through the door.

Nn

N is for nest
With baby birds inside,
The teddies like to watch them
As they are learning how to fly.

Oo

O is for owl
Sleeping in a tree;
The teddies must not wake him up
So they sit quietly.

Pp

P is for picnic
With lots of things to eat;
And all the teddy bears agree
It is a special treat.

Qq

Q is for queen,
Rosie pretends to be;
She sits upon her golden throne
For all her friends to see.

Rr

R is for river,
Flowing to the sea;
Fishing can be lots of fun
The teddy bears agree.

Ss

S is for sandcastle,
Ben builds by the sea;
Sam and Rosie want to help
And soon there are three.

Tt

T is for trumpet
All the teddies hear,
The trumpet playing loudly
As the band marches near.

Uu

U is for umbrella
To keep us dry from rain;
The teddy bears take cover
Until the sun comes out again.

Vv

V is for violin,
Polly plays a tune;
The others tap their feet,
They'll all be dancing soon.

Ww

W is for wigwam,
The teddies build for fun;
They like to look like Indians
Playing in the sun.

X is for xylophone
Rosie likes to play;
Her friends all sing together
As Rosie taps away.

Yy

Y is for yacht,
The teddies sail away;
They like to float around the lake
On a sunny day.

Zz

Z is for zebra,
He gallops round and round;
Sam and Polly watch him
As he runs along the ground.

1

One teddy bear is cycling.
The wheels turn round and round;
Up the hill, then down again,
He races all around.

2

Two teddy bears are in the park,
There's lots to see and do,
They swing and slide all morning
Then play ball all afternoon.

33

Three teddy bears are by the sea,
The sun is warm and bright;
When they have had their picnic lunch
They like to fly their kite.

3

Four teddy bears are gardening,
They help to clear the weeds;
There is a lot of work to do
Before they plant their seeds.

4

Five teddy bears are skipping,
The rope turns round and round;
They count each jump they make,
As they skip along the ground.

5

39

Six teddies like to rollerskate
Together in the sun;
Up and down the path they go
Having lots of fun.

40

6

Seven teddy bears are climbing
High up in a tree;
They reach the top, then look around,
There is so much to see.

7

43

Eight teddy bears are cleaning,
There is a lot to do;
They dust and clean and polish,
Working the whole day through.

8

Nine teddy bears play in the snow;
They like to skate and slide
Together down a snowy slope;
They all enjoy their ride.

9

Ten teddy bears are warm in bed
The moon is shining bright.
They like to hear a story
In the middle of the night.

10

Cycling

The teddy bears are cycling,
The wheels turn round and round;
They like to race each other
As they ride along the ground.

Running

All the teddies have a race
They're running very fast;
Rosie is the winner
And Polly comes in last.

Swimming

Swimming in the afternoon
Is what Rosie likes the best;
She races Ben and Polly,
Then has to stop and rest.

Jumping

Altogether in the rain
The teddies want to play;
Jumping in the puddles,
Splashing all the way.

Gardening

The teddies work together
There's gardening to do;
Sam and Ben are weeding
And Rosie's helping, too.

Shopping

Shopping in the afternoon
Is always lots of fun;
The teddies buy the food they need
Then walk home in the sun.

Swinging

The teddy bears are swinging
Together in a row;
They have to hold on very tight
As higher up they go.

Reading

Reading in the midday sun
Under the big oak tree;
"Look at the pictures, Sam," says Ben,
"We can learn our ABC."

Baking

Polly and Sam are baking
A special birthday treat;
Chocolate cake and cookies
Which they all love to eat.

Painting

The teddies are painting pictures,
They're having lots of fun;
Blue is for the sky above
And yellow is for the sun.

Skating

The teddy bears are skating
Together in a row;
They like to hold each other's paws
As down the ice they go.

Hiding

One teddy plays a game for fun
Hiding behind a tree;
He counts to ten and looks around
To find the other three.

Skipping

Skipping in the garden
The ropes go round and round;
The teddies count, "One! Two! Three!"
As they jump off the ground.

Climbing

Climbing high up in a tree
The teddies stop to rest;
They like to watch the baby birds
Sitting in their nest.

Sliding

Playing in the snow is fun
The teddies all agree;
When sliding down a snowy hill
As quickly as can be.

Dancing

The teddies all like dancing
To the songs they know;
Rosie plays the violin
As round and round they go.

Washing

The teddy bears are washing;
The day is nearly through;
Together they all wash and splash
And clean their teeth, too.

Sleeping

The teddy bears are all in bed,
They are sleeping tight;
And through the bedroom window
The stars are shining bright.

67

Jack and Jill

Jack and Jill went up the hill
To fetch a pail of water;
Jack fell down and broke his crown,
And Jill came tumbling after.

Up Jack got and home did trot,
As fast as he could caper,
He went to bed, to mend his head
With vinegar and brown paper.

Mary, Mary, Quite Contrary

Mary, Mary, quite contrary,
How does your garden grow?
With silver bells and cockle shells,
And pretty maids all in a row.

Ring-a-Ring o'Roses

Ring-a-ring o'roses
A pocket full of posies,
A-tishoo! A-tishoo!
We all fall down.

Baa, Baa, Black Sheep

Baa, baa, black sheep,
Have you any wool?
Yes sir, yes sir,
Three bags full;
One for the master,
And one for the dame,
And one for the little boy
Who lives down the lane.

Wee Willie Winkie

Wee Willie Winkie runs through the town,
Upstairs and downstairs in his night-gown,
Rapping at the window, crying through the lock,
Are the children all in bed, for now it's eight o'clock?

Old King Cole

Old King Cole
Was a merry old soul,
And a merry old soul was he;
He called for his pipe,
And he called for his bowl,
And he called for his fiddlers three.

Every fiddler, he had a fiddle,
And a very fine fiddle had he;
Twee tweedle dee, tweedle dee, went the fiddlers.
Oh, there's none so rare
As can compare
With King Cole and his fiddlers three.

Diddle, Diddle, Dumpling

Diddle, diddle, dumpling, my son John,
Went to bed with his trousers on;
One shoe off and one shoe on,
Diddle, diddle, dumpling, my son John.

Pat-a-Cake, Pat-a-Cake

Pat-a-cake, pat-a-cake, baker's man,
Bake me a cake as fast as you can;
Pat it and prick it, and mark it with B,
Put it in the oven for baby and me.

Mary had a Little Lamb

Mary had a little lamb,
Its fleece was white as snow;
And everywhere that Mary went
The lamb was sure to go.

It followed her to school one day,
That was against the rule;
It made the children laugh and play
To see a lamb at school.

And so the teacher turned it out,
But still it lingered near,
And waited patiently about
'Til Mary did appear.

Why does the lamb love Mary so?
The eager children cry;
Why Mary loves the lamb, you know,
The teacher did reply.

Little Jack Horner

Little Jack Horner
Sat in the corner,
Eating a Christmas pie;
He put in his thumb,
And pulled out a plum,
And said, "What a good boy am I!"

Little Miss Muffet

Little Miss Muffet
Sat on a tuffet,
Eating her curds and whey;
There came a big spider,
Who sat down beside her
And frightened Miss Muffet away.

One, Two, Buckle my Shoe

One, two,
Buckle my shoe;
Three, four,
Knock at the door;
Five, six,
Pick up sticks;
Seven, eight,
Lay them straight;
Nine, ten,
A big fat hen;

Eleven, twelve,
Dig and delve;
Thirteen, fourteen,
Maids a-courting;
Fifteen, sixteen,
Maids in the kitchen;
Seventeen, eighteen,
Maids in waiting;
Nineteen, twenty,
My plate's empty.

Little Tommy Tucker

Little Tommy Tucker,
Sings for his supper:
What shall we give him?
White bread and butter.
How shall he cut it
Without a knife?
How will he be married
Without a wife?

See-Saw, Margery Daw

See-saw, Margery Daw,
Jacky shall have a new master;
Jacky shall have but a penny a day,
Because he can't work any faster.

Sing a Song of Sixpence

Sing a song of sixpence,
A pocket full of rye;
Four and twenty blackbirds,
Baked in a pie.

When the pie was opened,
The birds began to sing;
Was not that a dainty dish,
To set before the king?

The king was in his counting house,
Counting out his money;
The queen was in the parlour,
Eating bread and honey.

The maid was in the garden,
Hanging out the clothes,
There came a little blackbird,
And snapped off her nose.

Ride a Cock-Horse

Ride a cock-horse to Banbury Cross,
To see a fine lady upon a white horse;
Rings on her fingers and bells on her toes,
And she shall have music wherever she goes.

Little Boy Blue

Little Boy Blue,
Come blow your horn,
The sheep's in the meadow,
The cow's in the corn;
But where is the boy
Who looks after the sheep?
He's under a haystack,
Fast asleep.
Will you wake him?
No, not I,
For if I do,
He's sure to cry.

Little Bo-Peep

Little Bo-peep has lost her sheep,
And can't tell where to find them;
Leave them alone, and they'll come home,
And bring their tails behind them.

Then up she took her little crook,
Determined for to find them;
She found them indeed, but it made her heart bleed,
For they'd left their tails behind them.

Jack be Nimble

Jack be nimble,
Jack be quick,
Jack jump over
The candle stick.

Twinkle, Twinkle, Little Star

Twinkle, twinkle, little star,
How I wonder what you are!
Up above the world so high,
Like a diamond in the sky.

When the blazing sun is gone,
When he nothing shines upon,
Then you show your little light,
Twinkle, twinkle, all the night.